My First Book about
Foxes
Amazing Animal Books
Children's Picture Books

By Molly Davidson

Mendon Cottage Books

JD-Biz Publishing

Read More Amazing Animal Books

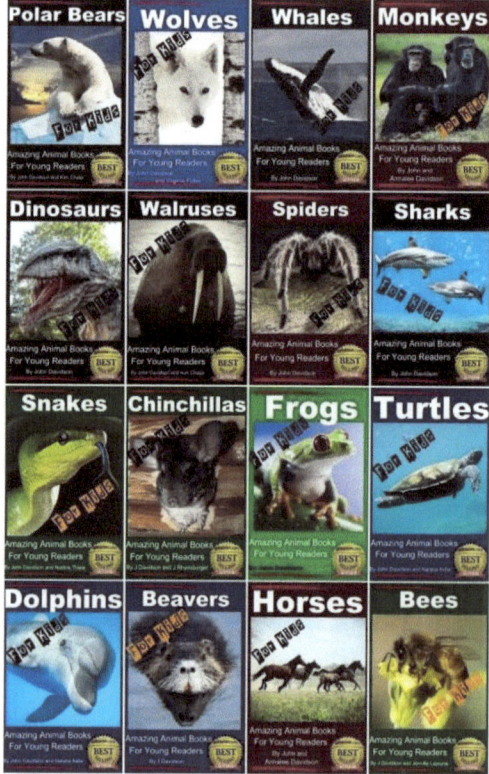

Purchase at Amazon.com

Download Free Books!

http://MendonCottageBooks.com

Table of Contents

Introduction...4

About Foxes...5

Characteristics..7

Foxes in different folklore and mythology.............9

Red Fox..11

Gray Fox..13

Arctic Fox...15

Fennec Fox..17

Kit Fox...20

Swift Fox..22

Bengal Fox..24

Silver Fox...26

Crab-Eating Fox...28

South American Gray Fox.............................30

Bat-Eared Fox...32

Hoary Fox...34

Tibetan Sand Fox..37

Conclusion..40

Publisher..47

Introduction

When you think of a fox, do you think they are sneaky and tricky?

Did you know foxes show lots of love, attention, and care for their babies?

Let's learn more about these animals called fox.

About Foxes

Foxes are mammals belonging to the family of Canidae.

They are omnivores; they eat both plants and meat.

Most fox have a bushy tail, triangular ears, a flat head, and a long nose, called a snout.

Foxes' special eyes allow them to hunt at night.

Their eyes are long and skinny, not round like many other animals.

Fox have claws that they can pull back into their paws, like a cat.

They don't chew their food; they just chunk it up before swallowing.

Humans hunt fox for their beautiful fur.

Characteristics

Fox are small compared to other four legged wild animals, like wolves, dogs, and jackals.

Girl fox are called vixens and boys are called dogs or tods or reynards.

Fox can live up to 10 years in the wild, but most die after about 2 - 3 years.

Fox live in small family units.

They pounce on their prey it makes for an easy kill.

Two species of fox, the Gray fox and Raccoon Dog, can climb trees.

Foxes in different folklore and mythology

Red fox are in many folklore tails, around the World.

In Greek mythology, there was said to be a huge red fox, which could never be caught.

In a Celtic tail, witches would turn themselves into fox to go steal butter from their neighbors.

In Korea, fox spirits which have nine tails are called "Kumiho."

In Peru, the Moche people worship the fox and foxes are found in many of their art pieces.

Red Fox

The Red Foxes are considered to be the largest among foxes.

They live in Central America, Asia, the Arctic Circle, and North Africa.

They like to hunt early in the morning or later in the evening.

They eat mainly mice, birds, reptiles, and sometimes vegetables and fruits.

Red fox can actually be red, silver/gray, black, brown, or a mixture.

They are hunted by large cats (like the bob cat), wolves, jackals, and coyotes.

They live in burrows that they dig in hills, bluffs, mountain slopes, ditches, and ravines.

Gray Fox

These foxes live in the region between south Canada and northern South America.

They used to be the most common fox, but too much fur trapping killed many of them.

They eat rats, rabbits, mice, and many vegetables.

Gray Foxes like to hunt at night.

They yap when they bark.

Gray fox are the only fox that is able to climb trees.

They live about 6 - 10 years in the wild.

Arctic Fox

The Arctic fox is also known as the polar fox, white fox, and snow fox.

They live in the arctic, mainly Alaska, where it is cold; this is why they have such thick fur.

Arctic Foxes' fur will change from white in the winter to brown in the summer.

They eat seal pups, fish, voles, and seabirds.

They have very good hearing; they can hear animals under the snow. When they find them, they will dig super fast until they reach them under the snow.

Fennec Fox

Fennec fox is also known as the desert fox and is the smallest among all fox.

They live where it is hot, in the Sahara Desert, which is in North Africa and Asia.

Fennec foxes' have very long tails, which have a black tip.

Their large ears help keep them cool, and well as help them hear animals under the sand.

They eat lots of plants, birds, reptiles, insects, rodents, and eggs.

The eagle owl is the main predator of the fennec fox.

Kit Fox

Kit foxes live in Nevada, Arizona, Utah, Texas, and California

A kit fox is grey, with some light brown, and dark black on their backs and around the nose.

They usually hunt small animals like cottontail rabbits, hares, insects, fish, snakes, dogs, meadow voles, and prairie dogs.

If food is hard to find, they will eat cactus fruits, tomatoes, and other fruits.

The kit fox lives in underground dens, which helps keep the cool in the summer and warm in the winter.

Swift Fox

Swift foxes are closely related to kit foxes.

They live in Colorado, Oklahoma, Montana, Texas, and New Mexico.

The swift fox is grey, with tan and yellow fur on their sides, with black patched on their nose. Like many fox, they also have a black tip on their tail.

They eat birds, lizards, insects, rabbits, ground squirrels, mice, and sometimes fruit and grass.

They are fast runners reaching speeds of over 30 mph to 40 mph. That is why they are called the "swift" fox.

Bengal Fox

Indian Fox <u>Wikimedia Commons</u>

The Bengal fox is also called the Indian fox.

They live in India, the Himalayas, Bangladesh, and Pakistan, mainly in forests.

 Bengal foxes build dens with many chambers and escape routes.

They eat insects, reptiles, crabs, rodents, small birds, termites, and fruits.

Silver Fox

Silver foxes are a type of red fox, they are different because of a color mutation.

They are dark grey or black with white on the tail.

Silver fox are most valued for their fur in China, Russia, and Europe, where they are worn as clothing often.

Silver foxes use scent marking, which shows other fox who's in charge and where food is.

Silver fox like to eat meat, but if they cannot find any, they will eat plants.

On Indian totem poles, silver fox are often carved.

Crab-Eating Fox

Crab – eating fox live mostly in South America.

They like tropical forests, shrubbery, woodlands, and tropical plains.

Crab-eating Fox <u>Wikimedia Commons</u>

They eat crabs (of course), birds, lizards, insects, eggs, fruit, and tortoises.

The crab-eating fox is mainly greyish brown with red legs and face. Their ears and tails have a black tip.

<u>Wikimedia Commons</u>

Their tail will stand straight up when they get excited.

South American Gray Fox

The South American Gray Fox is also called the Chilla, Patagonian fox, and Grey Zorro.

They live in South America, mostly in Chile and Argentina.

Their fur is grey with light grey underneath; they have long bushy tail and big eyes.

Wikimedia Commons

They eat fruits, frogs, bird eggs, scorpions, insects, seeds, berries, frogs, and lizards.

Bat-Eared Fox

The Bat- Eared fox is also known as the cape fox, big eared fox, Delalande's fox, and black eared fox.

They live where it is dry, in savannah's, and in Africa.

The teeth of a Bat- Eared Fox are really small and perfectly for eating termites, their favorite food.

Bat- Eared Foxes are fast, and can quickly get back to their den when faced with danger.

Rock pythons, leopards, jackals, African wild dogs, cheetahs, and spotted hyenas are their predators.

<u>Wikimedia Commons</u>

Their ears help them in listening to the sounds made by insects underground, it's just their way of finding more food.

Hoary Fox

Wikimedia Commons

Hoary Fox is also referred as Hoary Zorro and small toothed dog.

They live in Brazil; in bush lands, woodlands, and mountainous savannahs.

<u>Wikimedia Commons</u>

Hoary foxes are grey with a light grey under body, and reddish legs and ears.

"Hoary" literally means white; so they get their name from the white markings on their face.

They eat termites, grasshoppers, small birds, fruit, and rodents.

Tibetan Sand Fox

**An illustration of a Tibetan fox Alere Flammam.
1890 <u>Wikimedia Commons</u>**

Tibetan sand foxes are small in size and have soft
and thick fur coats.

They are mostly grey, with some tan on their neck, nose, and legs.

Their tails are bushy, and it has a white tip.

These foxes live in Tibetan, the Ladkh Plateau, Bhutan, India, and Nepal.

<u>Wikimedia Commons</u>

They hunt during the day, and live by themselves.

Tibetan fox eat rodents, pikas, lizards, woolly hares, blue sheep, antelope, deer, marmots, and sometimes livestock.

Conclusion

I hope you have loved reading about fox and can now go teach others about these wonderful animals.

Download Free Books!

http://MendonCottageBooks.com

Purchase at Amazon.com

Website http://AmazingAnimalBooks.com

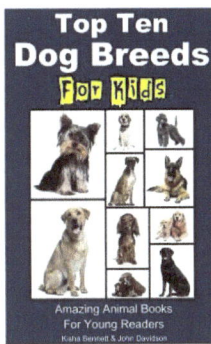

Top Ten Dog Breeds For Kids

Amazing Animal Books For Young Readers
Kisha Bennett & John Davidson

German Shepherds

Dog Books for Kids
K. Bennett

Bulldogs

Dog Books for Kids
K. Bennett

Dachshund

Dog Books for Kids
K. Bennett

Poodles

Dog Books for Kids
K. Bennett

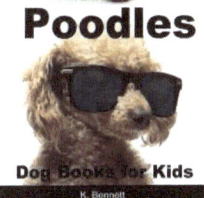

Labrador Retrievers

Dog Books for Kids
K. Bennett

Rottweilers

Dog Books for Kids
K. Bennett

Boxers

Dog Books for Kids
K. Bennett

Golden Retrievers

Dog Books for Kids
K. Bennett

Puppies
Dog Books For Kids

Amazing Animal Books
By John Davidson

Beagles

Dog Books for Kids
K. Bennett

Yorkshire Terriers

Dog Books for Kids
K. Bennett

Dogs
Top Ten Dog Breeds For Kids

Amazing Animal Books
For Young Readers
Zalva Jazeel & John Davidson

Cats For Kids

Amazing Animal Books
For Young Readers
K. Bennett & John Davidson

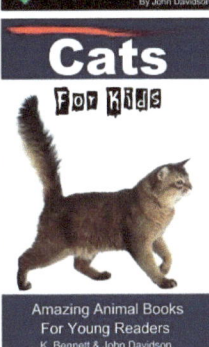

Foxes For Kids

Amazing Animal Books
For Young Readers
Zalva Jazeel & John Davidson

Wolves For Kids

Amazing Animal Books
For Young Readers
By John Davidson and Virginia Fidler

Our books are available at

1. Amazon.com

2. Barnes and Noble

3. Itunes

4. Kobo

5. Smashwords

6. Google Play Books

Download Free Books!

http://MendonCottageBooks.com

Publisher

JD-Biz Corp

P O Box 374

Mendon, Utah 84325

http://www.jd-biz.com/

www.ingramcontent.com/pod-product-compliance
Lightning Source LLC
Chambersburg PA
CBHW050837290526
45792CB00001B/434